LITTLE MI WINE O'CLOCK
AND FRIENDS
A Very Unofficial Parody

Little Miss Wine O'Clock is staying in tonight with her friend Little Miss Prosecco.

They are re-watching Downton Abbey and are playing a game called "Downton the Hatch". This means they have to sip a drink every time Lady Mary raises her eyebrows. Or whenever anyone opens a letter with a knife. Or whenever Carson clears his throat.

With the complete box set to watch it will be a long and messy night.

Little Miss New Year's Resolution has joined a gym.

On Monday, she overslept and missed her "Spin to Win" class. On Tuesday she forgot her sports bra for "Box-fit-or-Bust". On Wednesday "Extreme Hula Hooping" made her head spin. On Thursday she struggled to stand up straight during "Ninja Death Stretch".

On Friday, she decided the gym wasn't for her. Oh well, back to popcorn and "Poldark".

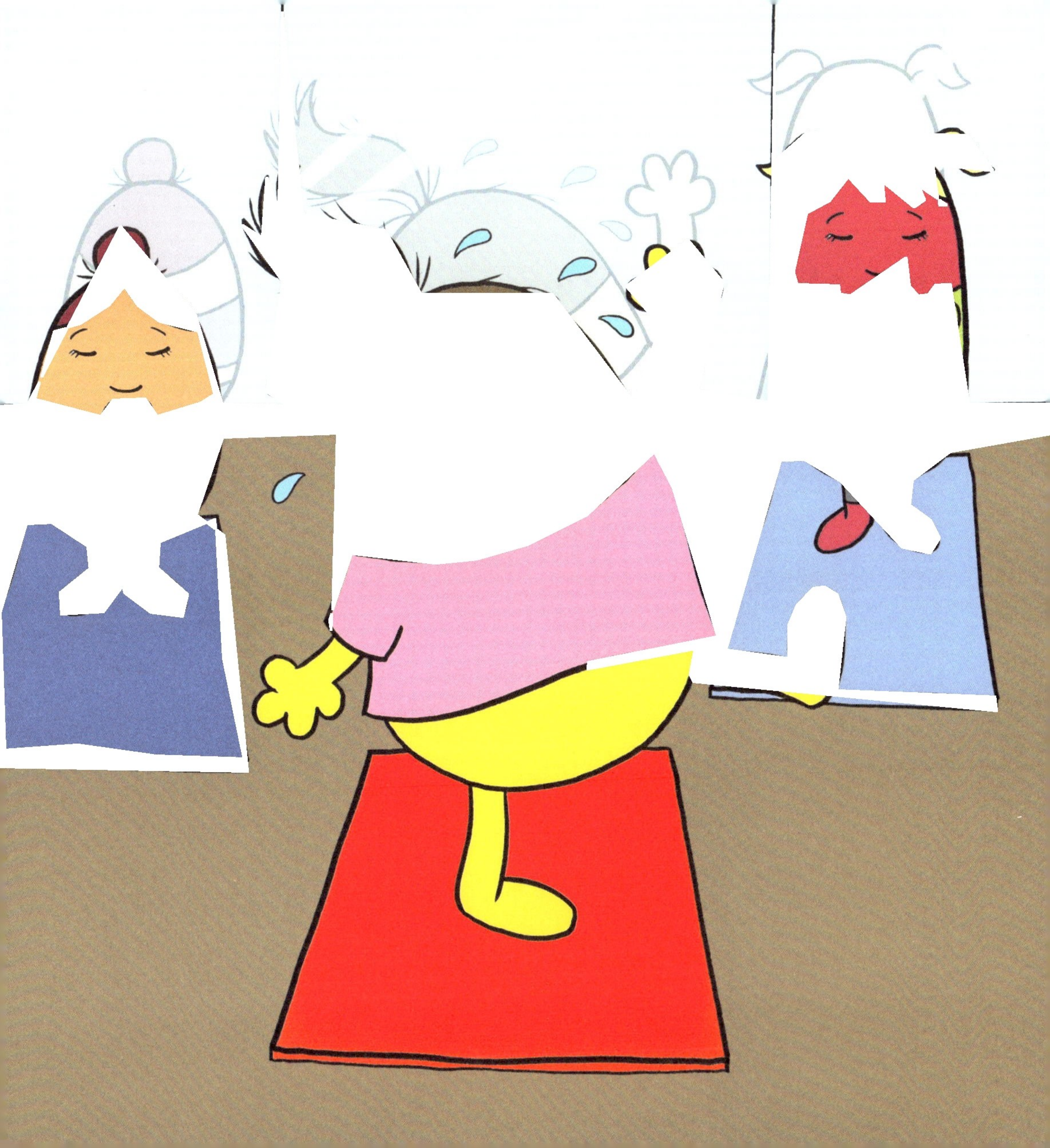

Little Miss Extreme Detox is on a kale-only diet.

She's trying to be healthy, if she could just stop thinking about CAKE. She uses mindfulness to help. She closes her eyes and visualises how tasty each mouthful of kale is. How, instead of limp and chewy, it is deliciously moist. Just like CAKE.

Wow! This kale doesn't even taste like kale anymore, it's lemony and buttery and… oh dear.

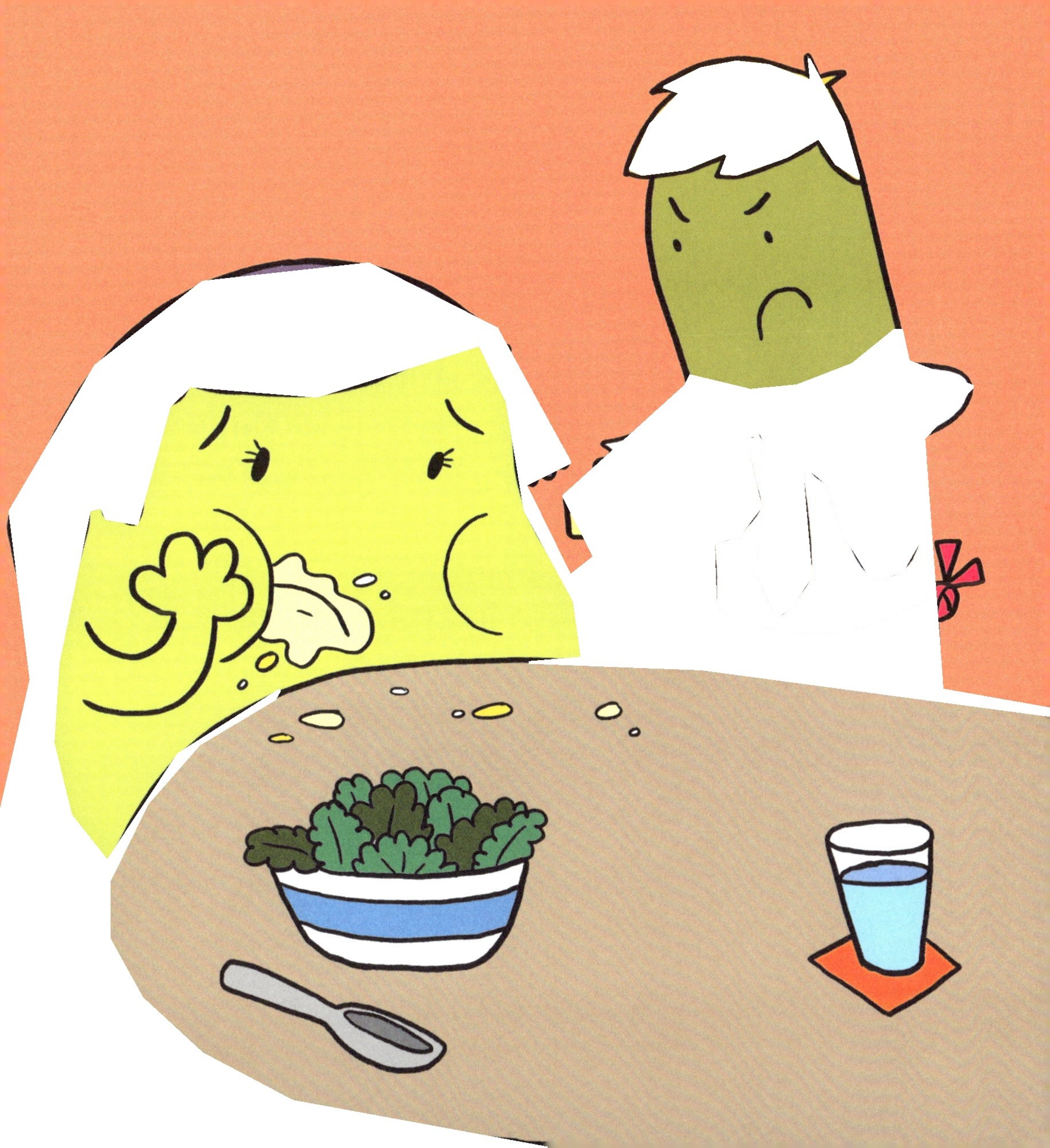

Little Miss Commuter lives in a train carriage.

Or at least, it feels like she does. Every morning she wedges herself into a packed carriage to spend two-and-a-half hours standing in a stranger's personal space.

She owns a lovely house in the country, but doesn't spend much time there as she is always travelling to and from work to pay for it.

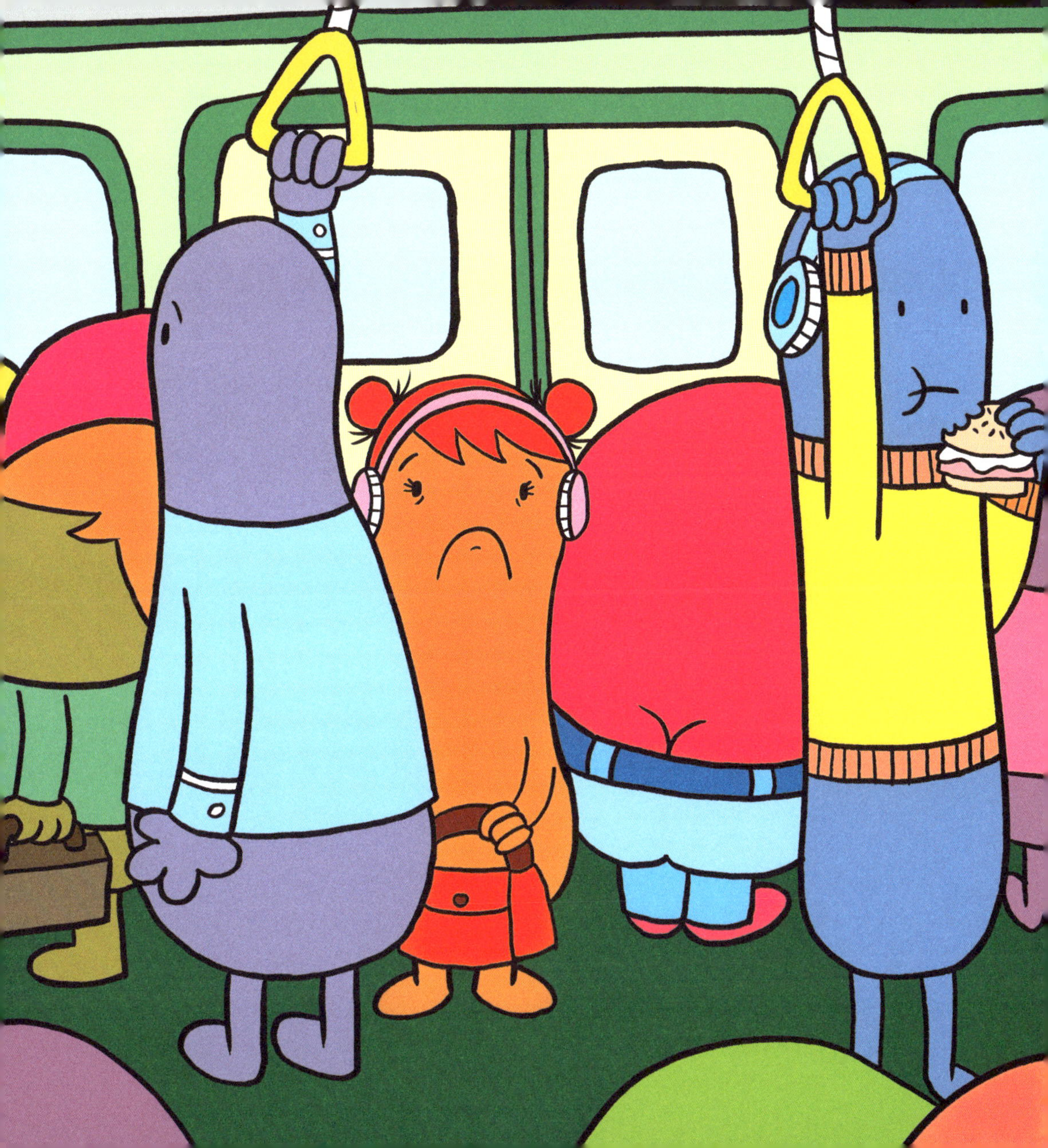

Little Miss Vintage is on the edge of her seat.

The online auction for the 1950s china is about to end. She increases her bid by 20p. She MUST have that new (old) tea set. Once, Little Miss Vintage was devoted to the 1940s, but it's all about the 1950s now.

She spots an ad for a gorgeous pair of 1970s shoes. Little Miss Vintage isn't sure she can pull off the 1970s. She looks terrible in brown.

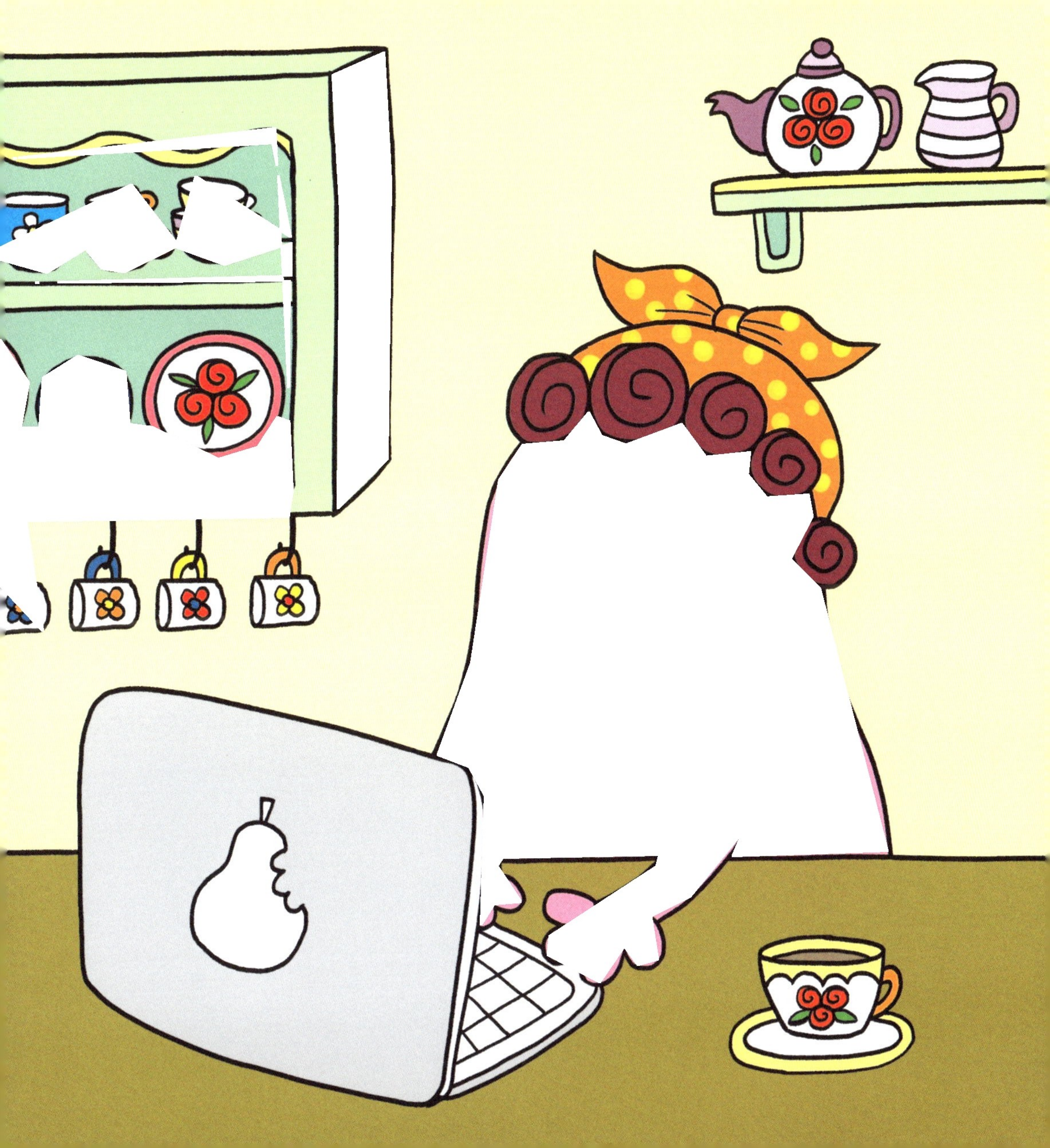

Little Miss Mombie used to go out, then she had children.

Now she mostly lives in her sitting room and spends most of her time picking things up.

Occasionally, she tries to leave the house. Once, on a very exciting Wednesday she made it as far as Sainsbury's, but had to come home because her baby projectile vomited over the fish counter.

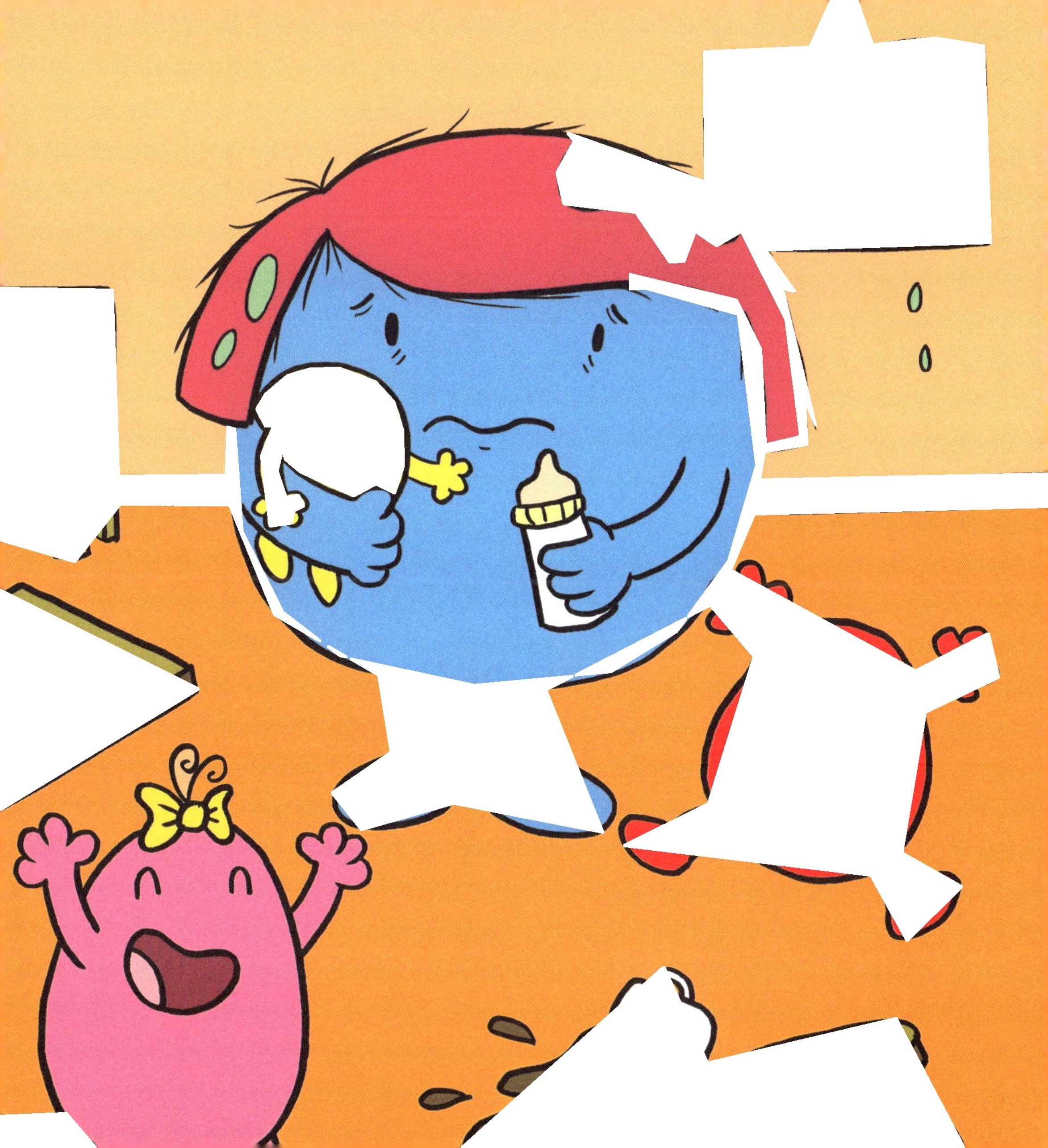

Little Miss Bridezilla wants everything to be perfect on her special day.

She's asked her bridesmaids to organise a low-key hen do trekking over the Andes, to dye their hair to match her colour scheme and to find a unicorn for her to ride down the aisle on. She hasn't asked them for much.

Thank goodness she has given up work to focus on the wedding full-time. She can't wait to tell her fiancé.

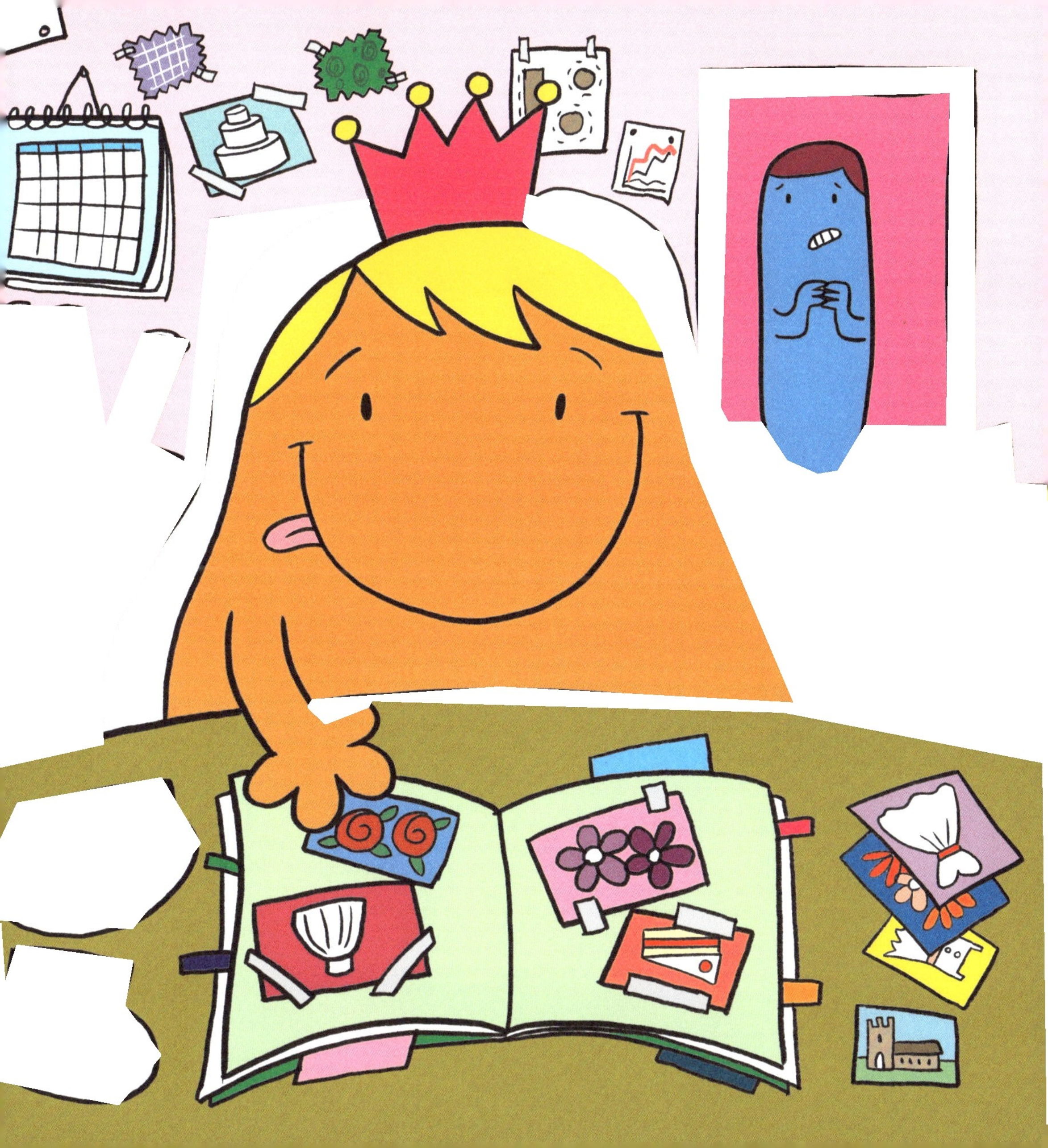

Little Miss Break-Up loves her new single life.

She has so much more me-time. She doesn't have to wash her hair as often, or shave her legs. She feels really empowered.

She's decided that she wants to learn some new skills, like felt-making, or learning Mandarin or Ancient Greek. Perhaps she'll even take up tae kwon do, or taxidermy. Something that's really fulfilling. That'll show him.

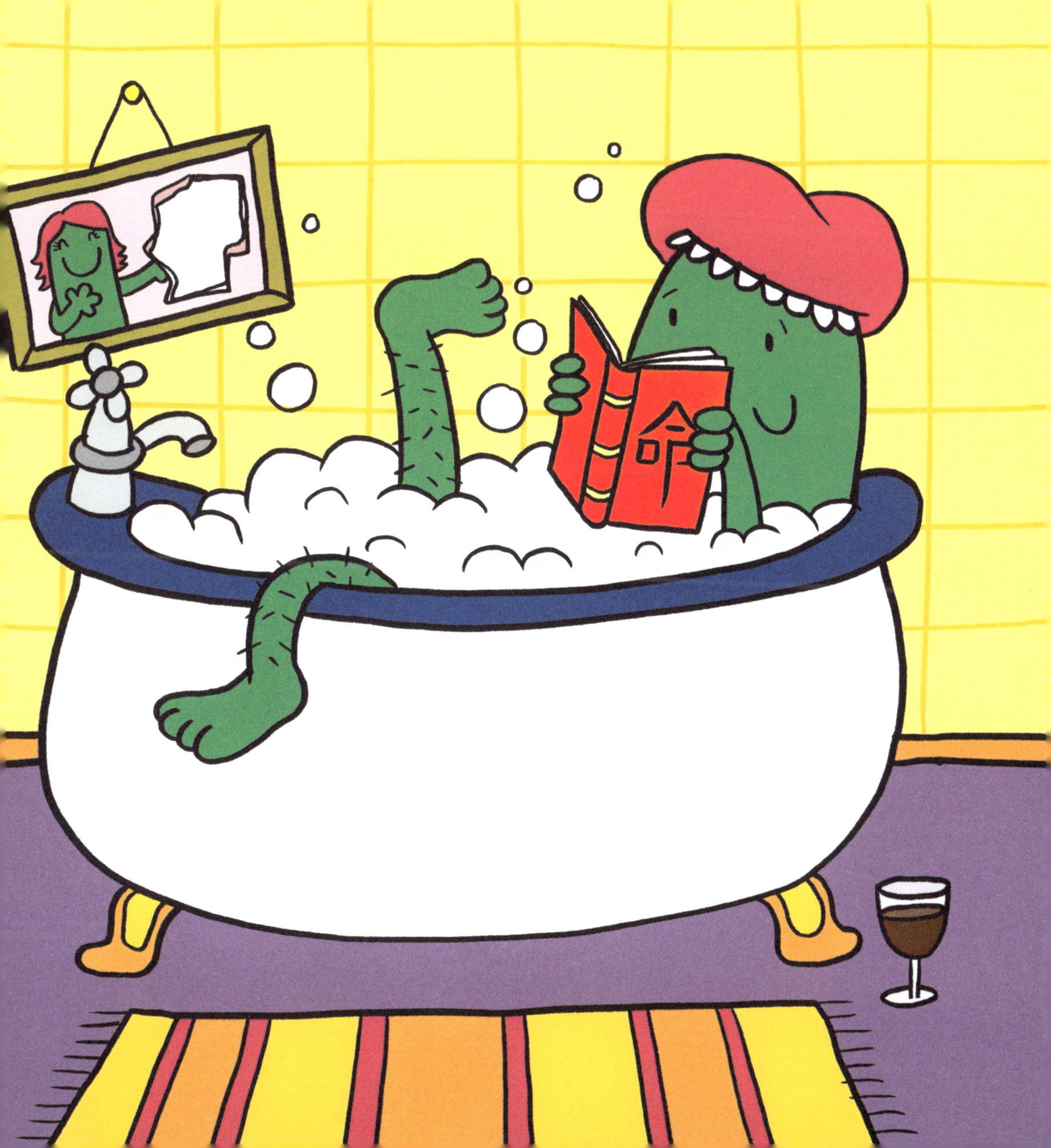

Little Miss Social Media does not understand why everyone is angry.

Don't people realise how important it is for her followers to be a part of her life? OK, so maybe not at Great Aunt Edna's funeral. And, on reflection, live streaming her BFF's harsh break up was probably not the right thing to do.

But a selfie? The actors should be thanking her. She's sharing and advertising their play for free. To all four of her followers. #sorrynotsorry.

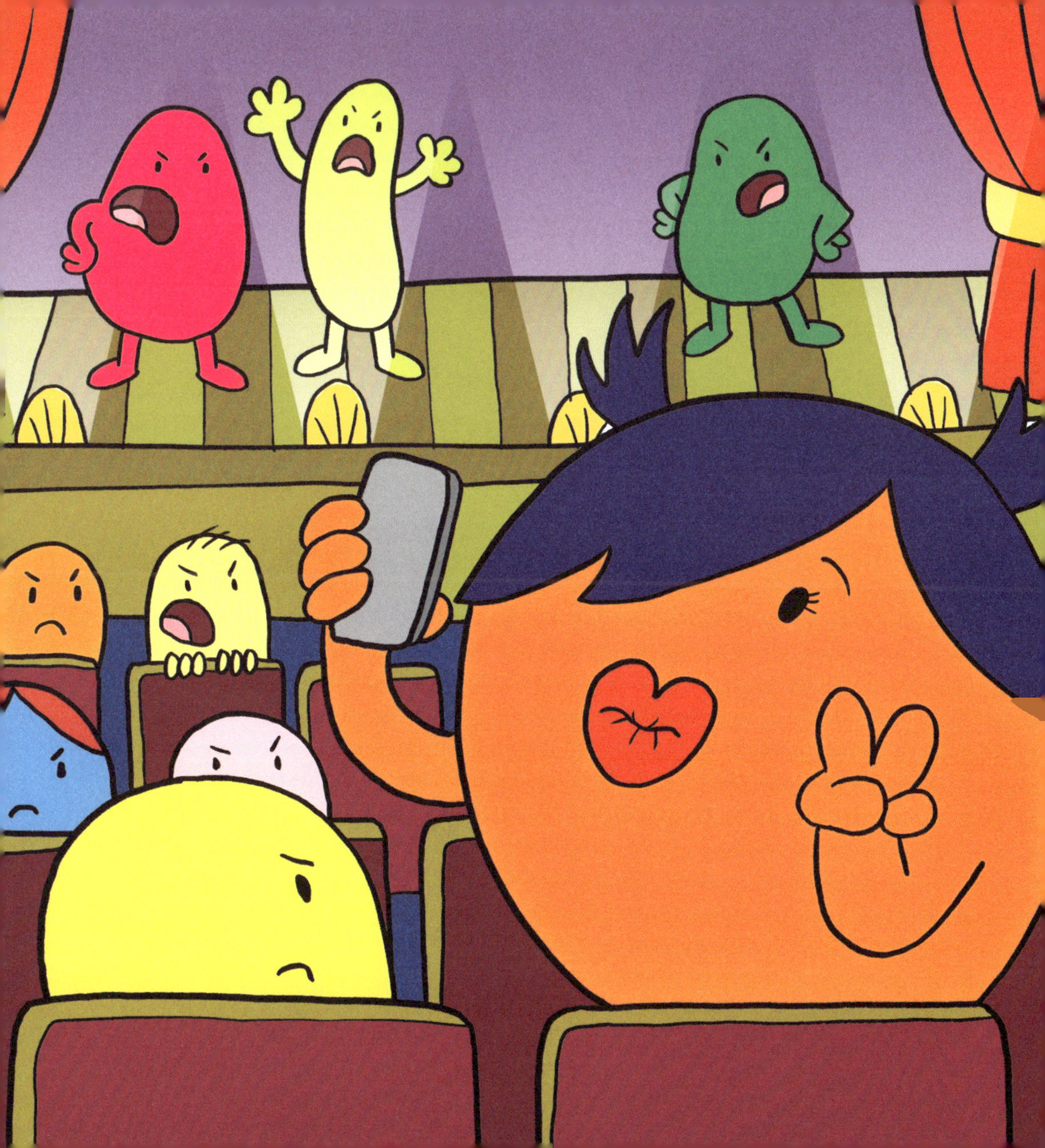

Little Miss Pushy Mum wants her children to be the best.

On Monday, they have bagpipe lessons followed by croquet. On Tuesday, it's medieval English then forest survival school. Wednesday is quite a tricky day, as all three children have to be in four different places at once. Little Miss Pushy Mum can achieve this by walking through walls.

It will all be worth it when her children get into the best nursery school.

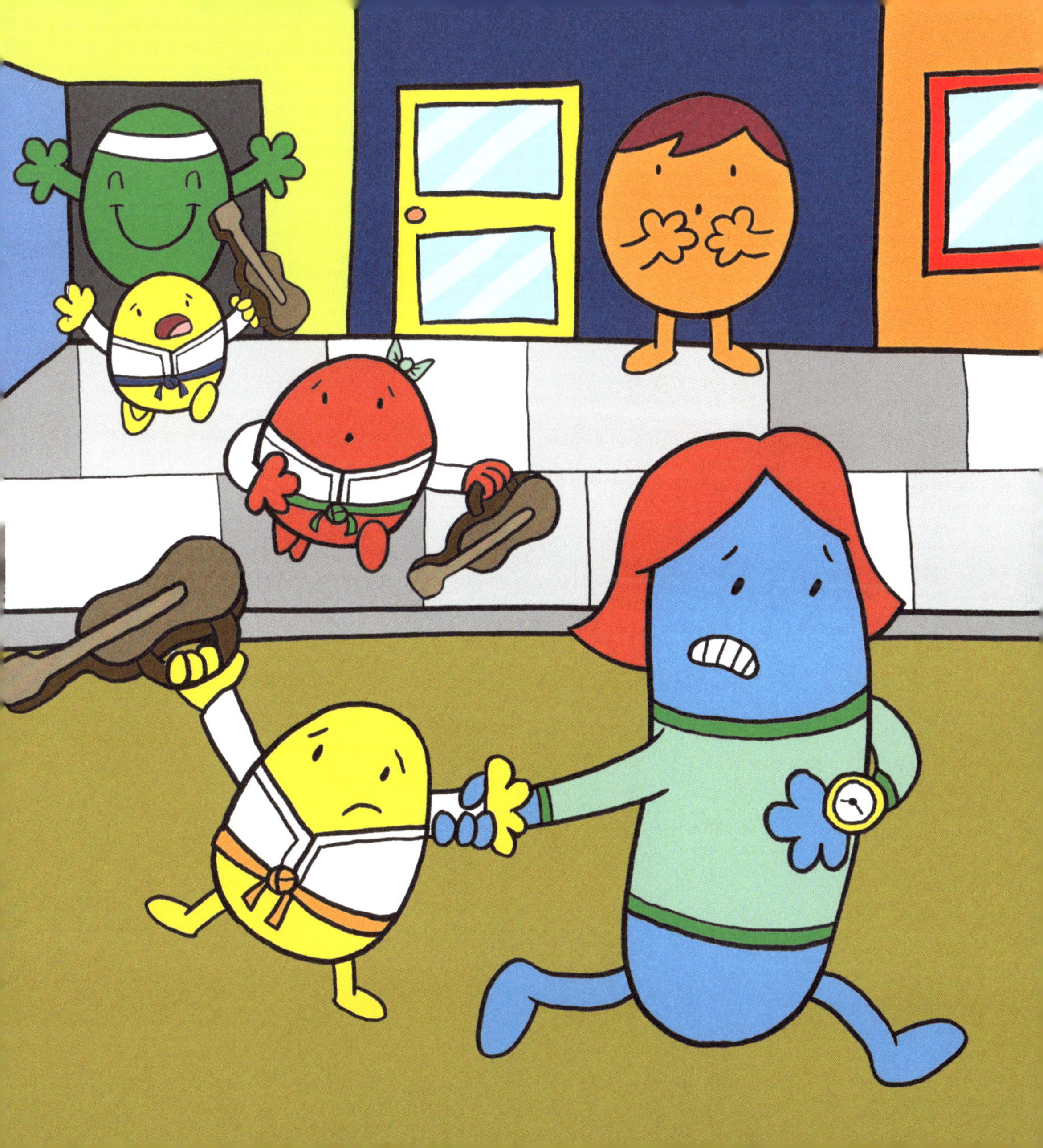

Little Miss Cat Lady is not crazy.

She does have A LOT of cats. Cats are much nicer than people. Come to think of it she does like cats more than she likes people.

People won't sit on your lap while you stroke them – not the people you want to sit on your lap, anyway, like that lovely Benedict Cumberbatch.

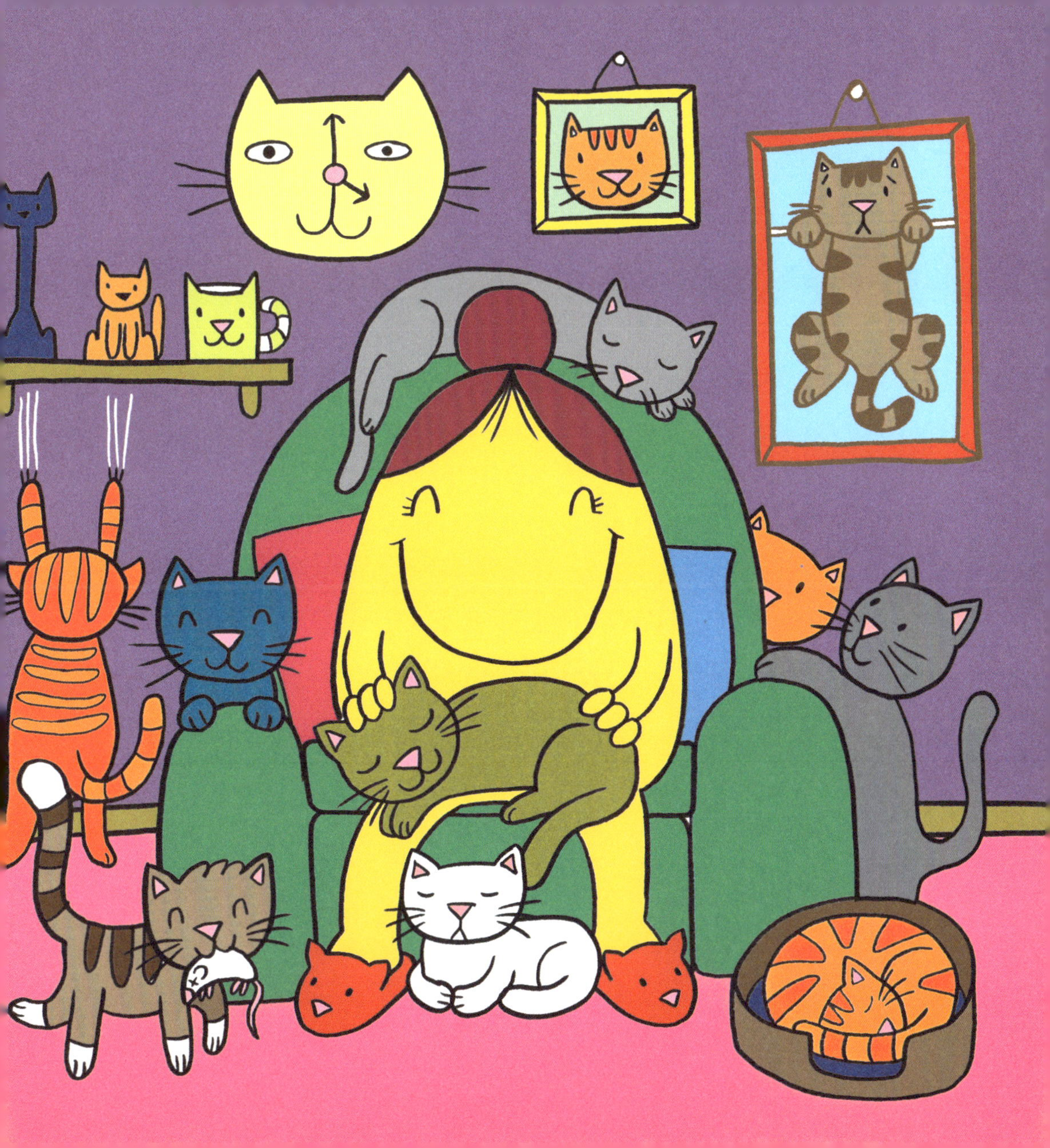

Little Miss Marathon is SO excited!

It is only four days until the next marathon – her fifteenth this year, and it's only February. Time to start rustling up some sponsorship money! She knows how much her friends love supporting her.

Although this morning the street seems quiet and strangely empty... where is everybody?

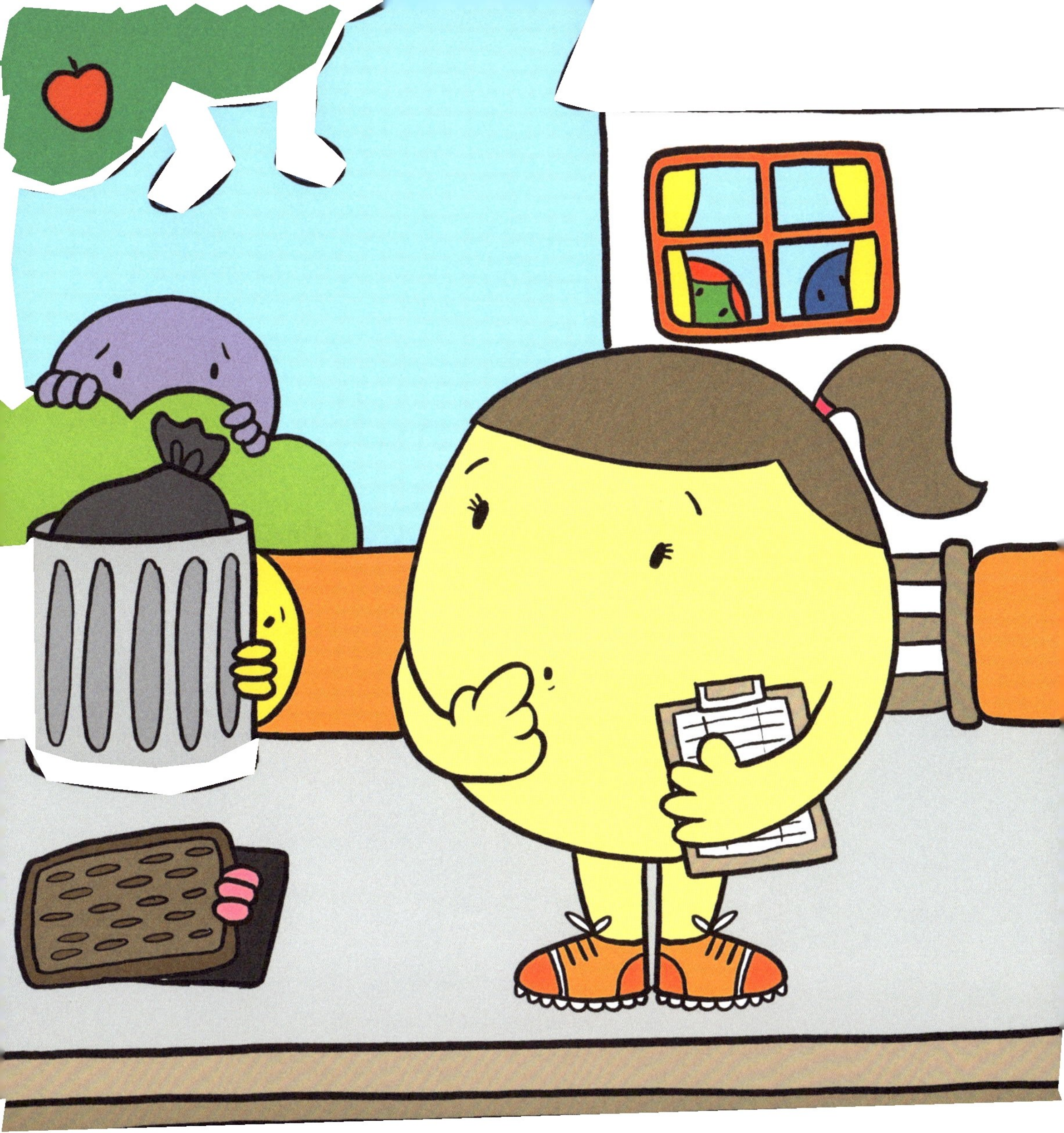

Little Miss Yummy Mummy loves her children.

She doesn't get to spend that much time with them as she's so, so busy with shopping and pilates and coffee mornings and things like that. Thankfully, they have the most wonderful nanny.

Actually, where is Nanny? If she doesn't turn up soon, Little Miss Yummy Mummy will have to take the children to school herself, and she's not entirely sure where it is.

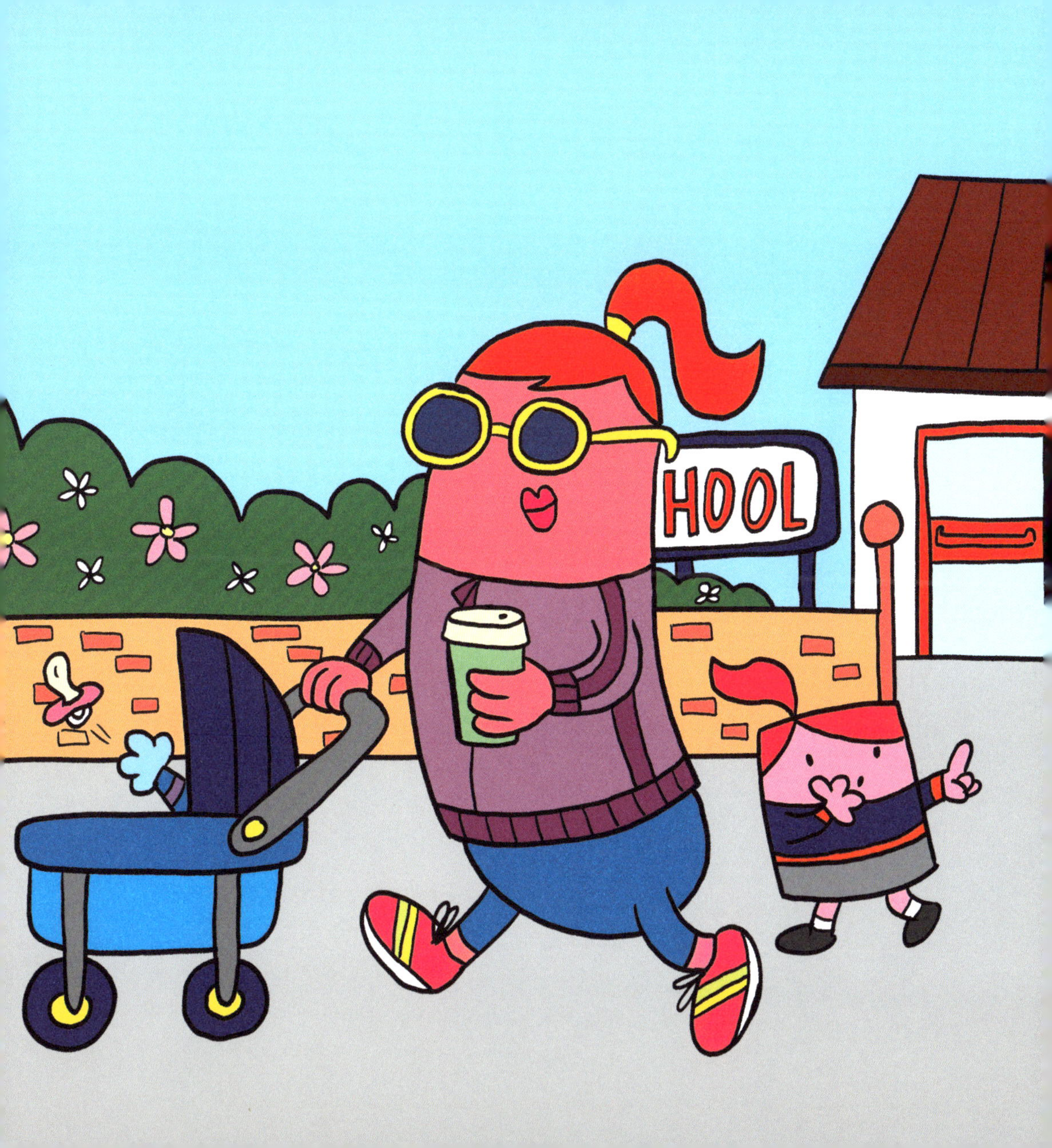
HOOL

Little Miss Botox hasn't had any work done.

Well, just a sprinkling of Botox here and there. Nothing really major. Now she thinks about it, it has been a while since she was able to smile, or frown, or raise her eyebrows… or move any part of her face at all.

Little Miss Botox doesn't consider this a problem. She can point to emojis to show her feelings.

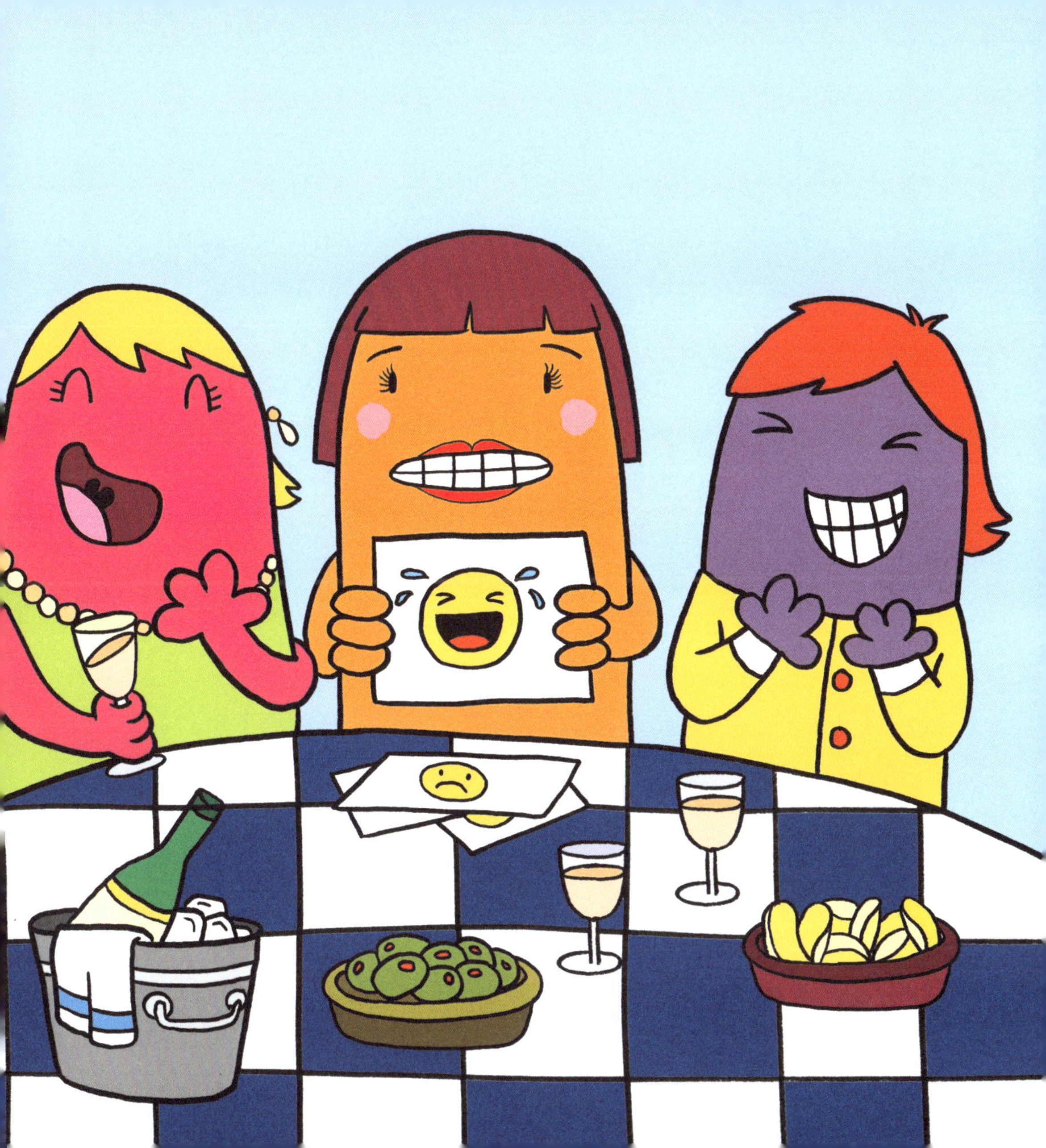

Little Miss Single is on an Internet date.

She is trying to be positive, even though Alan is not the wealthy human rights lawyer he said he was on his profile. He is in fact an office assistant who won't stop talking about his ex-girlfriend, Mavis. Little Miss Single can't think of an excuse to leave, so she stays. And pays.

Next time, she is going to do it the old school way and chat up someone on the train.

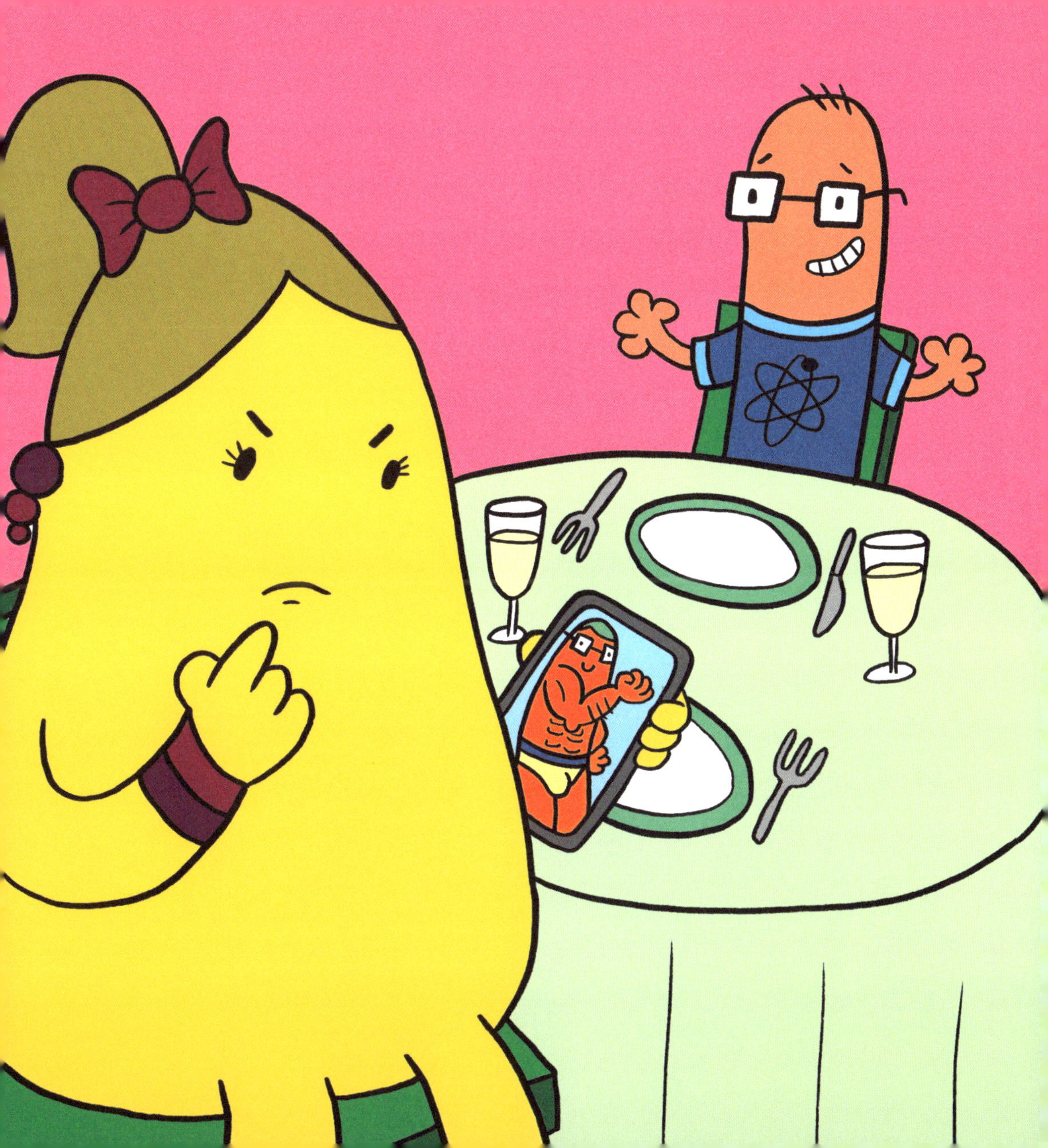